A journey through grief

Pam Robinson

BookLeaf
Publishing

India | USA | UK

Presentation by *BookLeaf Publishing*

Web: www.bookleafpub.com

E-mail: info@bookleafpub.com

ISBN: 9789358315257

First edition 2024

To Nige

*You are forever in our thoughts and dearly
missed.*

*You are loved beyond words and still a huge
part of our lives.*

ACKNOWLEDGEMENT

First off, I have to thank Elly Crew who gave me the nudge I needed to embark on this 21-day poetry challenge. You always were a bossy "so and so" with no respect for a Head Teacher!

To my family and friends who have offered endless support, patience and encouragement, especially my "Berrynarbor" family. A particular mention too to Jenny, Sue and Debs who always intuitively know when I need a phone call!

Finally, and most especially thanks to my daughters, Kate & Jess who went through all the emotions with me when the bottom had fallen out of our world and gave me the strength to keep going.

PREFACE

After losing my husband, I found solace in expressing my feelings through rhymes. I probably couldn't list the range of emotions I experienced at that time, if I tried. Words, particularly rhymes, flowed into my head, often in the middle of the night. This book is the outpouring of those rhymes and the outpouring of my grief. Over the last three months, I have realized there is no "one" way to grieve and there is certainly no "right" way. We are all so very different and it is OK to do things your way and in your time. My journey is probably far from over. I still have good days and bad but I am slowly learning to navigate a new path that is right for me.

"Stop, breathe and be still."

A journey

A journey through grief.
My journey, but sadly shared by, oh so many.
I am hoping this can bring some relief
for you and for me, but we will wait and see.

Sometimes it's good to know you're not losing
your mind.
Knowing others feel the same, is reassuring to
find.
Feelings -one minute so raw. Your heart oh so
sore
and yet another, you're fine, feeling guilty,
drinking wine.
We may wear different suits and travel different
routes.
The distances may vary too.
But the terrain is the same whatever your name.
Obstacles and challenges to pass through.
A journey of bewilderment, shock, confusion,
and disbelief,
interspersed with bouts of relief.
It may take a while; first face loss, anger, denial.
Dark, dismal days, feeling fierce, fiery rage
until your mood changes and you turn the page.

Sadness recurs from day to day- never truly
going away
But your heart slowly lightens as the horizon
brightens
Bringing comfort and relief from pain.
Whilst life will never be the same, you learn to
live again.

Come walk with me, I hope you can relate
to my journey laid before you.
My emotions laid bare, but I wanted to share
And hope they bring comfort and reassurance
too.

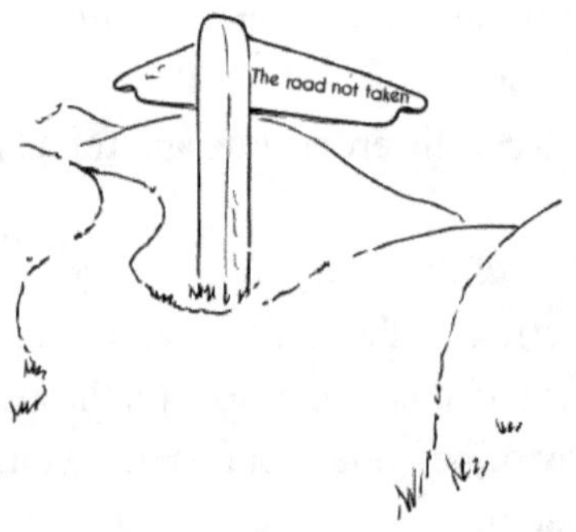

The Sea

As the sun rises on another new day,
I realize you're not here.
you've gone far, far away.
I feel lost and confused.
Are these really bad dreams?
Surely life is not how it now seems.

I walk out of our beach bungalow,
to where the sand meets the sea.
My body feels heavy; not really quite me.
The ocean rises and falls,
creating a racing, white foam.
I stand teetering on the edge,
feeling sad and alone.

The noise is quite deafening,
as the waves crash and roar.
Rushing up on to the land,
where I stand remembering before.
The sea pulls and pushes
churning up the sand.
My heart feels broken
as I twist my wedding band.

This was a happy place
with you by my side,
but so much has altered
now you've gone and died.
I want to hold onto the memories
of good times in this very sea;
Laughing and loving
with you close to me.
But right now I feel I am breaking in two
I'm not sure how I can manage life without you.

Emotions

It's only a week but it feels like a year.
Why am I struggling to find one single tear?
I want to cry out but nothing will come.
I want to hide away. Then I want to run.
I want to scream. I want to shout
What is life really all about?
Outside I've adopted a strange facade.
I must appear very, very hard.
I feel so numb with anger and pain.
Will I ever feel normal, like me once again?

My emotions keep changing all of the time.
One minute I am broken, the next I am fine.
One minute I am smiling, laughing, having fun,
remembering the special things that you said or
done.
I wish someone could tell me how I am
supposed to feel.
I wish someone could tell me none of this is real.
Is there a right way to feel right now?
Is there a right way to behave? Tell me how.
I really want to do right by you.
Someone tell me what I should do.

The painful truth

The truth is slowly settling in
you have truly gone.
Life will never be the same
from this time, from now on.

You were taken too quickly.
So hard to comprehend.
I have lost my right arm,
My co-conspirator, my one great friend.

How will I manage without you,
waking alongside me?
Not sure what the future holds
I'll have to wait and see.

They say that time is a healer.
I'll grow stronger day by day.
For now, I want to grieve for you,
And shut myself away.

But daylight has come, a new day is here.
I have to leave my bed.
Stop reminiscing on our happy times,
on the lovely life we led.

Put on my armour, face the world.
Accepting what comes today.
Slowly, realizing in my heart
You've truly gone away.

The truth is slowly settling in
You have truly gone.
My life must take a different path
Without you from now on.

Why?

There will be no answer to the question of why.
Why oh why, they were taken so early and
allowed to die?
There is no explanation as to when it's
someone's time.
No specified date on a contract to sign.
It just happens without our consent.
With no real opportunity to process and lament.
We just have to accept it and try to move on.
Acknowledging the void that's there when
they've gone.
An enormous space; a stone in your heavy heart.
Disbelief and regret that they have had to depart.
But keep returning to the memories you hold
dear
And that special loved one will remain quite
near.
Celebrate the short time you spent together.
That way you keep them alive in your mind
forever and ever.

The Funeral

Today's the day we say goodbye
I'm feeling very anxious, I cannot lie.
How will this day unfold?
What will the next few hours hold?

I pray the girls and I will cope;
Not too many knots and tears, I hope.
A positive send-off is all we ask;
Beautiful, fragrant flowers on a wooden cask.

Memories and moments with you we'll recall.
The impact you had on one and all,
Who come today to pay their last respect,
The little things you did with great effect.

Hopefully we've thought of everything.
So whatever today might go and bring
It's a celebration remembered by everyone
Of the things in life that you have done.

Today's the day we say "Auf Wiedersehen,"
Until of course we meet again
But for now, while we're apart
We'll enjoy all these memories living in our
heart.

Procedures

It's become a mountain of paperwork
Since you've been gone.
Umpteen questions checking I've done no
wrong.
Processes and procedures are the name of the
game.
Truly nothing is ever going to be the same again.
I thought I was a reasonably resilient girl
But as the weeks started to unfurl
I questioned my ability to truly cope
With the endless forms each day I wrote.
Without our daughters by my side,
staying strong, not thinking about their dad
who's died,
I probably would have simply slipped away,
Not continuing my own life another single day.
But for you and for them I know I must stay
strong.
Life for me really must go on.
I will fill in each form, follow the procedures too
I will do it for them, hopefully honouring you.

The joy of Friendship

As I sit at the dawn of another day.
I have so many feelings but so little to say.
I know once again I need to be strong
But it's hard taking each step, just carrying on.
Life can change in the flash of an eye.
A spirit here and then it must fly.
One minute it's sunny and then there's rain.
Things will never ever be the same again.
A new dawn, a new day.
Time to face whatever comes my way.
But a new day brings new hope.
With friends supporting me, I know I can cope.

Messages from others

So many people share our sense of loss
A special golfing partner, friend or boss.
It's wonderful to hear what they say about you;
They all realise you were special too.
Hard working, supportive and kind.
A better manager you'd struggle to find.
Good humoured, a great sport,
So many compliments, who'd have thought.
The messages certainly fill me with pride.
It's just a shame I didn't realise before you died.
So much we take for granted until someone's
gone.
I wish I had appreciated you more all along.

Counting time

I am a woman of words not numbers
and yet during my nights of fitful slumbers
I find myself counting the time spent with you.
Such a strange thing for me to do.

Last night whilst lying in a sleepy haze
I calculated we were together for exactly 38
years, 2 months and 4 days.
I remember the start and I remember the end.
Oh, how I wish, your heart I could mend.

To be exact, days together when you were alive
reached a grand total of thirteen thousand, nine
hundred and forty-five.
That's more than a life sentence, I hear you say
But I wouldn't have it any other way.

To be honest that's not entirely true.
I would have liked so much more time with you.
Instead the days and nights drag on.
There's an empty void now you have gone.

Reality is dawning

In the dead of the night
I wake with a fright
Realising you're gone forever.
It feels like a curse.
Things couldn't be worse.
Our life cut short together.

In the light of the day
I somehow find a way
To keep going alone, without you.
I'll grow stronger I'm sure
Storing memories and more.
What else is there I can do?

Grief

Grief isn't defined by race or gender.
It's an internal punishment for that lost love so
tender.
It's an angry beast that tears your insides out,
causing you to silently scream and shout.
It's a turmoil of emotions driving you slowly
insane.
An endless longing to see a face again.
It's loneliness beyond all understanding ever
experienced before.
It's blue, ice cold; feelings so raw.
It's a knife that stabs you in the dead of the
night,
Raising feelings that cause your body to fight.
It's painful, it's lingering; it won't go away.
It leaves emptiness and longing at the start of
each day.
As each morning dawns, I never forget
but I am slowly learning to not live with regret.
What happened has happened; the past can't be
changed.
Now it's up to me, my future can be rearranged.
I will move on forward, making the most of each
new day.
Living a different life, but living it my own way.

Losing control

Emerging emotions start to overwhelm
Causing me to question who's really at the helm.
I thought I was in control, managing just fine,
But then these feelings overtake me time after
time.

Utter sadness that life has changed so much.
Longing for the one I want to touch.
Disappointment for the plans we made together.
Disbelief that he has gone forever.

Anger, why is life so unfair?
Anxiety, will people cease to care?
Regret for the things I didn't get to say.
Loneliness which grows stronger day after day.

Negative emotions consistently wear me down.
Feel like I am suffocating, feel like I could
drown.
Tormented, miserable, unable to sleep.
All I can do now is sit here and weep.

Good and bad days

Some days everything seems against you,
no matter what you do.
The day starts in a troubled way and continues
all day through.

On those days it's hard to don the usual mask
you use to face the world.
Your mood is there for all to see.
Emotions are unfurled.

I'm learning it's OK to scream and shout and
allow the tears to flow.
It's OK to let your feelings out and allow others
to know.

Once the trouble passes and you feel in control
once more
You can get back to living, reopening the door.

Grief is a journey no one really wants to make.
It brings a mix of emotions; it's really hard to
fake.

Run with it if you can, it's like a roller coaster
ride.
It's a challenge one has to go through
to mourn the one who's died.

They say it will get better but I'm not sure it
really will.
The void of those who have gone away is really
hard to fill.

But we will wake up and keep on going as we
face another day.
Wishing in our heart of hearts they'd never gone
away.

Grieve in your own way

Just because I don't grieve aloud
Or wail from the highest tree.
Just because I prefer a crowd
than solitude; only me.

I may not appear sad enough
Or anxious just like you.
That doesn't mean my grief
is unreal or in some way untrue.

Reminiscing may bring me joy.
I may even recall a joke.
Laughing isn't really bad.
I'm just different from other folk.

My grief is mine and mine alone.
I will do it the way it feels right.
I can't pretend or perform just for others.
Try as, maybe I might.

Only I, alone, know how I feel
About what's really going on.
I know my life will never be the same
Now that he has gone.

My grief is different, but that's OK.
My tears you may not see.
We each cry in our own special way.
So, stop questioning and let me be!

Silence

Silence is golden or that's what they say.
For me it highlights your absence
in my life every day.

Silence is not golden, to me it is black.
It emphasizes the lack of your presence.
You're never coming back.

Silence is solitary.
It says I am alone.
Never again will you return home.

Silence is manageable,
Allowing time to think of you.
Happy memories have space to keep flooding
through.

Silence is yellow, it's green and it's brown.
Sometimes acceptable,
but sometimes causing an enormous frown.

Silence is hard, but comfortable too
arousing other senses.
Bringing me closer to you.

Silence is silence. I accept that in the light of day.
Acknowledging what I can't change
driving negativity away.

Time really is a healer

Getting up is becoming less hard.
Slowly life resumes.
No flowers today, not even a card.
Grief no longer consumes.

A new normal is settling in.
Days without you around.
No beer to pour, just one gin.
Is drinking alone now allowed?

I walk on my own but you're by my side,
giving me strength to carry on.
It seems so long since you collapsed and died.
Realizing you're not here; you have gone.

Reality hurts, but it's no longer raw.
You'll never again be here.
Things will never be the same as before
But I'll keep going; never you fear.

Today and tomorrow too

As tempting as it is to stay in bed
I need to brace myself and face the day ahead.
No longer two; a solitary one.
I am learning slowly, life can still be fun.

Seize the opportunities that come along each
day.
Doing what's best for me in my own special
way.
I have turned a new page; it's going to be alright.
The future looks different but I can make it
bright.

Understanding Loneliness

Loneliness is not age related
At any time it can creep up and leave you
feeling tainted.
The child in the playground playing all alone
Pretending he's fine when he gets back home.
The teenager hiding behind emo trends,
Frustrated and angry through lack of true
friends.
The new mum, struggling each day with her
precious baby.
Once a high class banker and now a
stay-at-home lady.
Either parent when the offspring flee the nest.
Now their relationship is really put to the test.
They can sit side by side in their own front room
Like strangers all at sea with emotions of doom.

The widow or widower when their loved one has died
Evenings spent longing they were back by their side.
Loneliness lives even in a room full of friends.
It's all-consuming power never really seems to end.
It segregates and isolates, pulling you apart
Causing throbbing in your head and daggers through the heart.
It's a sickening feeling that can't be subdued.
At its worst in the evenings the pain you can't allude.
It twists and twines from deep inside.
Causing anxiety and hurt; feelings that can't be denied.
A release may come from time to time
When you don a smile and pretend you're fine.
Reassure family and special friends too.
After all, what can they really do?
To others it's a simple feeling, never mentioned on the phone.
But to the sufferer it's a disease; an affliction to face all alone.

Life moves on

Today has been a good day,
That's all I can say.
Nothing extraordinary walking, cooking and
eating,
But it felt OK.
Stopping for a chat, challenging the mind.
Realizing faith is simply more than being kind.
Wondering where God is in events today,
But having the confidence to know things will be
OK.
Sometimes it's just about living and taking one day
at a time.
Appreciating life is good and things will be just
fine.
Not questioning why; simply letting life be.
Realising, it's going to be alright, I can simply be
me.
It's OK to cry but to laugh too.
It's OK to not wonder what you'd say or do.
It's not that I am forgetting or even moving on.
It's simply accepting you have really, truly gone.
Friendship and kindness I will wholly embrace.
My history no longer, a worry for me to retrace.
It's time to accept where I am right now.
Embrace each day, not questioning how.
Put one foot in front of another
and see what comes to pass.

Have confidence it's time to move on
but the memories will last.

Memories

Memories are precious they remind me of the
past
But now new memories I need to make
 that will also last and last.
A different life is mine to take
with ups and downs and the odd mistake
But I need to move forward doing things anew.
That doesn't mean I won't remember or will
even forget about you.
On the contrary, because of you I know I can be
strong.
The memories we made together keep me
moving on.

A new normal

Life is different without you
And yet so much is the same.
My home, my lifestyle
And even my name.
I get up, I go out. I walk the dog.
I eat and watch TV
Some nights I even sleep like a log.
Going about my new life day to day
There's no doubt I still miss you.
Living life in a new way.
One step in front of another
From morning until night
I will keep going
Although you are out of sight.
How can life go on when you have died?
How can days progress
Without you by my side?
And yet it does
Every day becomes a new normal
Things carry on; nothing formal.
This doesn't mean I love you any less.
Or I have forgotten you too soon.
It's just about me moving on.
Accepting I cannot live a life of doom.

Little steps of progress

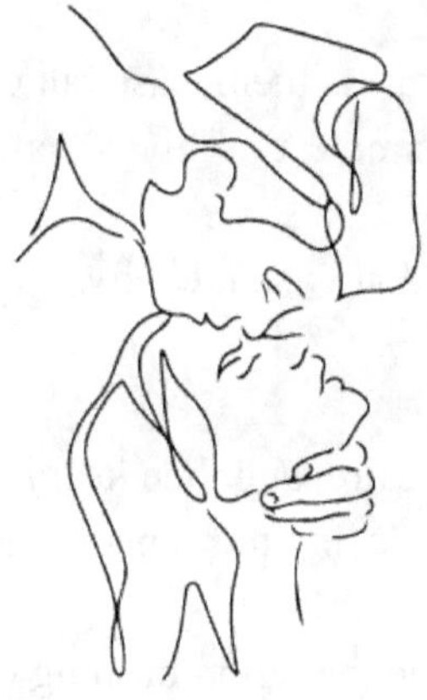

Can I tell you some things that may make you
smile?
Come sit with me, this may take a little while.
The tiny things accomplished slowly, day by day
since you died and left me; since you went away.
It's not been easy, I have to confess
But each day I grow stronger, and I worry less
and less
about the things that I can't do right now.
One day I know I will realise how.

There's been lessons to learn and feats to
perform.
A bit like a ship in a mighty big storm.
I have weathered the waves crashing over me.

The new challenges each day I sometimes don't
see.
Some days I'm bedraggled with the challenges I
face,
but I try to address them, case but case.
It's been the simplest of things that have caused
me to cry.
Crazy things don't ask me why.

Like starting a fire, and then keeping it going
Opening and closing the vents without really
knowing
how to stop the logs from burning too quick.
But I've cracked it now… well that's what I
think.
The TV devices really took some time.
Understanding the controllers were all truly
mine.
Flicking through channels all power in my hand
The workings of each, I don't truly understand.

The things in your shed I uncover week by
week.
Screws, nails and pliers I am beginning to seek.
That lawn mower of yours is truly a mean beast.
Cutting the lawn has been no mean feat.
My lines may be wiggly all over the place
and I picture the horror on your familiar face.

At least I have done it. I hope you approve.
No longer fearful of needing to move.

I have cracked paying bills and online banking
too.
It wasn't easy as that job was for you.
Passwords to remember, it's not really my thing
But I am trying very hard to remember
everything.
All these tasks may take me quite a while
But I am getting there my love, you have to
smile.
I think you may watch over me from time to
time
Quietly reminding me these tasks now are all
mine.

I sometimes hear your voice even though you
have gone
Applauding and encouraging me to keep
carrying on.

Moving forward- Moving on.

Putting one foot in front of another.
Life resumes again.
Whilst exhausting emotions move you forward,
Your energy drains.

Some days are better than others.
You just don't really know
what each day will bring along.
Whether you will be high or you'll be low.

You keep on going because
you know you must.
Relying on some inner strength and
the friends, you know you can trust.

Time is a great healer
or so they say.
Your ability to manage improves
day by day.

Keep going and be kind to yourself.
It's what you now must do.
Slowly, slowly you evolve
into the sad, but new you.

Life has changed forever
Things will never quite be the same
But the love you shared together
will certainly remain.

The garden

Today is going to be a good day.
"Are you sure of that?" I hear you say.
Well put it this way I will do my best.
"I know you will, I expect nothing less."

It's not the same without you here
"I know it's different but you have nothing to
fear
I am with you every day
Walking beside you every step of the way."

I want to see you, hold your hand
"But you can on our stretch of land.
Look at the steps I struggled to make
The mossy grass I toiled to rake.

I uncovered the water trickling down the hill
I see our boy drinks from it still.
The outdoor kitchen I created especially for you.
And the roof over the hot tub I built that too.

Those rhododendrons we planted together
They will grow strong and go on forever.
The veggie plot I created with love.
I will watch you plant from up above.

Sow me sunflowers that will grow so high
Perhaps I will touch them here in the sky
It's your turn now to do what you can
Come on, you're as good as any man!"

With you beside me I will do my best
"I wouldn't expect any less"
There's such a lot that I can do
And I'll do it knowing this time it's for you.

Being positive

Are you still with me?
You've been gone quite a while.
I still treasure our memories.
They continue to make me smile.

Come sit alongside me.
Let me feel you near.
Enjoying those memories,
We both held so dear

I recall each of the holidays
We spent together.
Laughing and loving
As though we had forever.

I am glad we didn't know
What was about to come.
Better to lack knowledge
Remaining completely dumb.

We enjoyed our time,
Living life to the full.
No "what's ifs" for us
Or doubts to over-rule.

Life was all good,
Filled with positive stuff.
We took it for granted.
Never appreciating enough.

Now it's all gone
I value what we had.
Giving thanks for the good times.
Those memories make me glad.

They warm me;
keep me going day by day.
Making life bearable
since you went away.

Come sit alongside me
Let me feel you near.
Enjoying those memories
We both held so dear.

The Chair

The chair sits alone on top of the hill
Unused and empty standing upright and still.
It tells a story of abandonment, loss and grief.
When it once was a special place, bringing
comfort and relief.

Your voice would ring out at the end of the day.
"I've done a good day of gardening, time for a
beer" you would say.
Together we would sit in silence or chatter,
Enjoying the view, the weather didn't matter.

Warm with companionship, simply enjoying life
without fuss.
No airs or graces simply us being us.
We enjoyed surveying our kingdom, our garden
to some.

Talked of our plans; of things yet to come.

Life was good, we were complacent back then
Not thinking of death, not realising when
Life would change in the twinkling of an eye
Not giving us the chance to really say goodbye.

But now…I will take up my place on that
abandoned chair
And recall the good times when I had you right
there.
I will return to its comfort with a beer in my
hand
And again survey the beauty of your garden, our
land.

I will treasure the memories when all is said and
done.
Raise a glass, live life and have a little fun.
Because unlike the chair unloved and left alone,
I can enjoy the beauty of the place we made our
home.

Our Happy Place.

North Devon captured us right from the start
With its golden beaches close to my heart.
You loved the local pub and the golf too.
There was so much to explore; so much to do.

We fell in love with our beautiful new home.
Confident in our dreams; no need to roam.
A love affair started to grow
As you cleared the weeds and new seeds you'd
sow.

The garden, your new challenge, brought you
much pleasure.
For me, I enjoyed it at my leisure.
You planted, you pruned, and your confidence
was regained.
Your delight in your achievements was never
feigned.

It makes me smile now each time I look out.
Your last years were your happiest, I have no
doubt.
The friends we made and the things we did
together.
Happy memories that will last forever.

People ask and wonder will I now move?
Why would I, when this place mends and
soothes.
This place brought us happiness, satisfaction and
love anew.
I will continue to grow here just like you.

The Anniversary

It's a year today since we said goodbye.
It's been up and down, I cannot lie.
Some days it feels like torrential rain;
Pelting hailstones, will I see you again?

Like a ship out at sea navigating a storm.
I rise and fall struggling to find a new norm.
I question what happened, try to understand your
health.
Most of this I keep to myself.

I hate the times you seem, oh so far away.
When your name's not mentioned or thought of
at least once in a day.
I strive to still make it, all about you.
Always hoping you approve of the things that I
do.

Other times I feel you right here at the heart.
It's as though we have never really been apart.
Those times are mainly when the girls are back
home.
Or we are chatting on the phone.

"What would dad make of this or that?"
"What would he have said if he could join this
chat?"
You are with us when we are laughing, having
fun.
And we'll make sure you're there in the
weddings to come.

As I walk the garden you are always by my side.
It's still very much yours even though it's
changed, since you died.
And on the beaches, looking out to sea.
You are always there appreciating, alongside me.

St David's Day has become your day too.
The day we said goodbye to you.
It's the day I will always acknowledge that you
have gone.
But slowly realise it's also ok to move on.

Love overrides death

White lace and wedding rings gifted.
Love is celebrated and hearts are lifted.
Blessed for a life of happiness together.
Happiness that should last forever and ever.
But life sometimes takes a different turn.
Events deviate, causing emotions to churn.
Sadness, anger, disappointment as love is
replaced.
Loneliness and confusion, the new emotions
faced.
Navigating each new day in a bit of a daze
but slowly, slowly you emerge from the haze.
You realize that the love hasn't gone
It can outlive death and truly live on.
Reliving the memories and the places you loved,
feels like a blessing sent from above.
A gentle reminder that love can last forever,
despite no longer being physically together.
There is no timeline on grief
But one day when it's right you find great relief.
Two rings can now combine to a heart
Demonstrating a love that will never depart.

Stairway to Heaven

If I could reach up to heaven
Just for one day
There are so many things I would like to say.
People and faces I long to see again.
It would be a real trip down memory lane.

To my parents gone now for far too long,
I would say sorry for all the times I didn't listen
to them and got things wrong.
I would thank them for the wonderful childhood
they gave me
And tell them of my achievements, knowing
they'd be as proud as can be.

To my sister I would hug with so much joy.
No longer the pain that just used to annoy
I would pour a wine and sit and tell
All about her children doing oh so well.

I can see her smile if I close my eyes
Delighting to hear about her special guys.
Her wonderful grandchildren, too young when
she passed;
Three boys and a girl all growing up fast.

To one special friend I would just hold tight.
So many tears I would have to fight.
But I know in heaven she won't need to fast.
In heaven she will surely be experiencing peace
at last.

And what would I say to my husband dear
What would I whisper in his ear?
Snatched away in the twinkling of an eye.
So many tears I have had to cry.

Why was he taken on that fateful day?
Why oh why is all I will say.
I will thank him for all the time we enjoyed
together
And remind him I will love him forever and
ever.

I will ask him to stay close to the girls and I
Never forgetting us as the days go by.
To ensure that we always feel him near,
sharing our happiness and drying the odd tear.

As I turn away from heaven it will be with a
heavy heart.
This time it's my turn to have to depart.
For I still have life back here on earth.
There's so much I need to do to appreciate its
worth.

I will hold onto my memories of those who have
passed;
Memories so precious that will endure and last.
But I will make the most of each and every day
Knowing when we meet again, I will have even
more to say.